HOW AWESOME CAN YOU BE?

BE CARING

by Emma Carlson Berne

Consultant: Beth Gambro
Reading Specialist, Yorkville, Illinois

Minneapolis, Minnesota

Teaching Tips

Before Reading

- Look at the cover of the book. Discuss the picture and the title.
- Ask readers to brainstorm a list of what they already know about caring. What can they expect to see in this book?
- Go on a picture walk, looking through the pictures to discuss vocabulary and make predictions about the text.

During Reading

- Read for purpose. As they are reading, encourage readers to think about showing caring in their own lives.
- Ask readers to look for the details of the book. What are the specific ways someone can be caring?
- If readers encounter an unknown word, ask them to look at the sounds in the word. Then, ask them to look at the rest of the page. Are there any clues to help them understand?

After Reading

- Encourage readers to pick a buddy and reread the book together.
- Ask readers to name two ways to be caring that are included in the book. Go back and find the pages that tell about these things.
- Ask readers to write or draw something they learned about being caring.

Credits:
Cover and title page, © kali9/iStock; 3, © shironosov/iStock; 5, © kali9/iStock; 6–7, © FluxFactory/iStock; 9, © LUNAMARINA/iStock; 11, © PeopleImages/iStock; 13, © kali9/iStock; 14–15, © MNStudio/Shutterstock; 16–17, © Maria_Usp/Shutterstock; 19, © Markus Mainka/Shutterstock; 20–21, © Goodboy Picture Company/iStock; 22TL, © zoranm/iStock; 22TR, © katleho Seisa/iStock; 22BM, © StockPlanets/iStock; 23TL, © M-Production/Shutterstock; 23TR, © Veja/Shutterstock; 23BL, © kiankhoon/iStock; 23BM, © ShineTerra/Shutterstock; and 23BR, © Africa Studio/Shutterstock.

Library of Congress Cataloging-in-Publication Data

Names: Berne, Emma Carlson, 1979- author.
Title: Be caring / by Emma Carlson Berne.
Description: Minneapolis, Minnesota : Bearport Publishing Company, [2023] |
Series: How awesome can you be? | Includes bibliographical references and index.
Identifiers: LCCN 2022031735 (print) | LCCN 2022031736 (ebook) | ISBN 9798885093224 (library binding) | ISBN 9798885094443 (paperback) | ISBN 9798885095594 (ebook)
Subjects: LCSH: Caring--Juvenile literature. | Etiquette for children and teenagers--Juvenile literature.
Classification: LCC BJ1475 .B464 2023 (print) | LCC BJ1475 (ebook) | DDC 177/.7--dc23/eng/20220819
LC record available at https://lccn.loc.gov/2022031735
LC ebook record available at https://lccn.loc.gov/2022031736

Copyright © 2023 Bearport Publishing Company. All rights reserved. No part of this publication may be reproduced in whole or in part, stored in any retrieval system, or transmitted in any form or by any means, electronic, mechanical, photocopying, recording, or otherwise, without written permission from the publisher.

For more information, write to Bearport Publishing, 5357 Penn Avenue South, Minneapolis, MN 55419

Contents

Awesome Caring 4

Showing Caring 22

Glossary 23

Index 24

Read More 24

Learn More Online 24

About the Author 24

Awesome Caring

Everyone needs help sometimes.

We can be there for one another.

Caring makes sure everyone is **supported**.

Being caring is awesome!

Being caring means thinking about how others are feeling.

It is giving them what they need.

Showing others you care makes everyone feel awesome!

Ask a friend what they are feeling.

Listen to what they say.

Learning about someone else's feelings is caring.

How else can you find out how someone is feeling?

Use **empathy**.

Imagine how you would feel if something happened to you.

Another person may feel the same.

Treat others how you would like to be treated.

Is your friend sad?

Try to cheer them up!

Is your brother happy?

Be glad for him.

How else can you be caring?

If someone is hurt, get them a **bandage**.

Ask if they would like a hug.

Do not forget about animals!

You can care for them, too.

Feeding your pets shows you are thinking about what they need.

Try **self-care**.

Eat a healthy snack.

Ask for help if you need it.

You can take care of others best when you are well.

Caring helps others.

It is one way to show how awesome you are.

Everyone needs caring sometimes!

Showing Caring

Care for your classroom.

1. Ask your teacher if they need help.

2. Make a plan to do a job for them.

3. Show your teacher you care by doing the job well.

Glossary

bandage a piece of cloth or tape put over a hurt part of the body

empathy the understanding for the feelings of another

imagine to picture something in your mind

self-care doing things for your own health

supported helped along

Index

animals 16
bandage 14
empathy 10–11
feelings 6, 8, 10
friends 8, 12
hug 14
self-care 18

Read More

Krekelberg, Alyssa. *Helping Friends and Family: Taking Care of Others.* Mankato, MN: The Child's World, 2020.

Nelson, Penelope S. *Having Empathy (Building Character).* Minneapolis: Jump!, Inc., 2020.

Learn More Online

1. Go to **www.factsurfer.com** or scan the QR code below.
2. Enter "**Be Caring**" into the search box.
3. Click on the cover of this book to see a list of websites.

About the Author

Emma Carlson Berne lives with her family in Cincinnati, Ohio. She tries to be a caring person to everyone!

24